HOW TO SURVIVE BEING A GRANDPARENT

A Hilarious Guide for Grandmas and Grandads

ILLUSTRATED BY
IAN BAKER

KATE FREEMAN

summersdale

HOW TO SURVIVE BEING A GRANDPARENT

Text by Colin "Cee Tee" Jackson

Illustrations by Ian Baker

An Hachette UK Company
www.hachette.co.uk

Summersdale Publishers
Part of Octopus Publishing Group Limited
Carmelite House
50 Victoria Embankment
LONDON
EC4Y 0DZ
UK

www.summersdale.com

This FSC® label means that materials and other controlled sources used for the product have been responsibly sourced

MIX
Paper | Supporting responsible forestry
FSC® C016973
www.fsc.org

The authorized representative in the EEA is Hachette Ireland, 8 Castlecourt Centre, Dublin 15, D15 XTP3, Ireland (email: info@hbgi.ie)

Printed and bound in China

ISBN: 978-1-83799-513-4
eISBN: 978-1-83799-514-1

INTRODUCTION

Congratulations!

How wonderful – you're a grandparent! This is a cause for celebration.

But just when you thought you'd have some time to yourself, your life is set to change dramatically. In case you'd forgotten, looking after an infant isn't easy! Why else would your own child be so keen to foist the little one on you?

Becoming a grandparent can be a daunting proposition; having fun with your grandchild while adhering to the stipulations of their parents is a delicate balancing act. Whatever your concerns, this book is here to teach you how to survive being a grandparent.

Cash in that savings plan, Granny and Grandpa! The first round of celebratory drinks is going to be expensive!

BAR

Be prepared – as a grandparent, you will be expected to be ready to look after Baby at a moment's notice.

Avoid nuclear-grade nappies by not feeding your infant grandchild on jars of prepared cauliflower cheese.

Get down "wit da kidz" by
donning your trendiest outfits
for that walk in the park.

CHERISH THAT ONE LINE YOUR VERY YOUNG GRANDCHILD IS GIVEN IN THEIR FIRST NURSERY SCHOOL NATIVITY PLAY.

BAAAA

BRRRRRINNNG
SCHOOL

Realize most
social interactions
will no longer be at
the pub, golf club or
coffee shop, but
at the school gates.

IT'S TRUE, COMICS ARE NOT AS GOOD AS BACK IN YOUR DAY – BUT THEY ARE STILL AN ENJOYABLE READ.

COMIC

You will at last find an appreciative audience for your terrible amateur magic tricks.

Despite what your child may say, it's your right – no, it's your duty – to spoil your grandchildren.

No matter how much you love them, the best thing about grandchildren is that you can hand them back.

You are undoubtedly an excellent bedtime storyteller. Perhaps, though, skip the bit about the monster living under the bed.

STORY
TIME

Eventually, even you
will be convinced that
unicorns and fairies exist.

TAKE ADVANTAGE OF THE FREE HELP IN THE GARDEN WHILE YOUR GRANDCHILD IS STILL ENTHUSIASTIC AND IMPRESSIONABLE.

TOTAL KNOWLEDGE
BOOK OF FACTS
ENCYCLOPEDIA

Grandchildren
expect you to know
the answer to every
question in the universe.
Best brush up on that
general knowledge!

WHILE GREAT FOR BONDING, WATCHING TELEVISED BAKING SHOWS TOGETHER WILL ONLY GIVE RISE TO LOFTY AMBITIONS.

To better appreciate your grandchild's perspective, it's helpful to adopt and immerse yourself in the imagination of a child.

Forget sudoku puzzles for keeping your mind active – remembering the names of those coming to tea is practice enough.

TED
DOLLY
BUNSIE

Steady, Grandpa!
It's been a few years
since you last stopped
a goal at any
level of football.

You will become familiar with your grandchild's ability to look cute and innocent, no matter what.

All presents from your grandchild should be gratefully received and treasured.

WHEN YOUR GRANDCHILD STAYS OVERNIGHT, IT'S PROBABLY BEST TO SUPERVISE THEM GETTING DRESSED FOR NURSERY IN THE MORNING.

Set your grandchild a good example by encouraging and demonstrating healthy eating.

BEWARE! THERE IS NO ONE BETTER ABLE TO WIND YOU ROUND THEIR LITTLE FINGER THAN YOUR GRANDCHILD.

LOVELY THINGS SHOP
£200.00

When the sign at the play park states, "Children over the age of 12 are prohibited", it doesn't include grandparents.

We all know you're your grandchild's number one fan – don't be afraid to show the rest of the world!

STAR
PUPIL
AWARD

GLUE
MODEL KIT

If you can help
your partner assemble
flat-pack furniture,
surely you can help
your grandchild build
a model aeroplane?

Demonstrate how cool and trendy you are by learning the lyrics to the latest hit by Taylor Swift.

FUN MAZE

Carefully select the venue
for a fun day out to
maximize time for yourselves.

IMPRESS YOUR TEENAGE GRANDCHILDREN BY TELLING THEM YOU USED TO "SPIN THE OLD ONES AND TWOS" BACK IN THE DAY.

PENGUINS

Don't take your eyes off young grandchildren on a visit to the zoo.

REMEMBER THAT GRANDCHILDREN ARE REMARKABLY RESOURCEFUL AND QUITE CAPABLE OF SOLVING PROBLEMS WITHOUT YOUR "HELP".

SUPERMARKET

Small grandchildren can prove very helpful assistants when you are doing the weekly supermarket shop.

If using Lego with your grandchildren, don't think it silly to count all the bricks back into the box.

Try not to discourage your grandchildren – after all, mud pies are delicious!

It's true – grandparenting is as easy as riding a bike.

Encourage your grandchildren
to benefit from your
vast experience and
knowledge of engineering.

GRANDCHILDREN WILL ALWAYS VIEW A VISIT TO YOUR HOUSE AS SOMETHING MAGICAL AND EXCITING.

Surprise teenage grandchildren by posting a TikTok video of you performing the latest dance craze.

ENCOURAGE YOUR GRANDCHILDREN TO SHARE YOUR PASSIONS.

TACKLE

Coax your grandchildren away from streams on their tablets and show them how streams provided entertainment in your youth.

AND YOU THOUGHT HELPING YOUR GRANDCHILDREN BUILD MODEL AEROPLANES WAS DIFFICULT!

PLANS

Don't forget one of
grandparenting's most
important rules:
bribery is everything.

It's good to encourage a competitive nature in your grandchild, but less becoming to exhibit one yourself.

20
20
100
20
100
5
5
5
10

BOUNCY
CASTLE
HAPPY
BIRTHDAY

There's nothing like a bit of friendly competition with the "other" set of grandparents.

Self-care is important – be sure to maximize your own nap time by synchronizing it with theirs.

ZZZZZZZZZ

HOW TO SURVIVE RETIREMENT

ISBN: 978-1-83799-511-0 · Hardback

ATTENTION ALL RETIREES!

This book is the essential guide to navigating life beyond the nine-to-five. Your freedom begins here and you're going to need all the advice you can get on how to while away the hours, make cool new friends and avoid total boredom. Charmingly illustrated, this tongue-in-cheek guide is packed with tips that will have you chuckling from page to page.

THE LITTLE INSTRUCTION BOOK FOR SENIORS

ISBN: 978-1-83799-371-0 · Hardback

It really is the life in your years that counts

Now that you're a senior, you'll come to realize that there is nothing that can't be fixed by a quick trip to the garden centre, that your "bad back" will reliably get you out of any tricky situation and that it's now socially acceptable to call anyone younger than you "Dear" rather than remember their actual name. In other words, now the real fun begins!

Encouraging you to laugh, embrace life and enjoy the ride, the pearls of wisdom in this no-nonsense handbook will guide you through all the pleasures and pitfalls of your senior years.

Have you enjoyed this book?
If so, find us on Facebook at
Summersdale Publishers, on Twitter/X
at **@Summersdale** and on Instagram
and TikTok at **@summersdalebooks**
and get in touch.

We'd love to hear from you!

www.summersdale.com